DIESES BUCH GEHÖRT:

www.ingramcontent.com/pod-product-compliance
Lightning Source LLC
Chambersburg PA
CBHW030015190526
45157CB00016B/2838